THERE'S

FIRE

IN YOUR MOUTH

Dr PATRICK ONORIE

THERE'S FIRE IN YOUR MOUTH

- "You don't know what kind of a spirit you belong to..."- Luke 9:55.
- "From the time of John the Baptist and until now, the kingdom of God suffereth violence, and the violent take it by force."- Matt 11:12.

Table Of Contents.

Acknowledgments

The Holy Spirit has been at the center of this project from the onset, and any acknowledgments should be ascribed to Him because of His inspirational ingenuity and the on-the-spot mentoring. Most times I hear the Holy Spirit dictates to me what I should put down; the speed and fluency of the work make me conclude so. When I tried to think of a topic of interest, He quickly joined me in my thoughts; when I prayed at the initial time before contemplating on areas of concentration, He speedily gave me eleven topics to write on within the first thirty minutes.

So, I concluded that the Holy Spirit is actually the brain behind this project; the speed is enormous, and He alone should receive all glory, honor, and majesty in Jesus' name, amen.

Preface

Most profound statements made by Jesus Christ in the scriptures are enclosed in this eBook, 'THERE'S FIRE IN YOUR MOUTH'; he said, "Ye know not what manner of spirit ye are of."-KJV. The GNV however rendered it in modern English as," You don't know what kind of a spirit you belong to..." Yes! This is a profound statement of truth, which goes to show that you are not an ordinary person; but do you know you are special specie? The underlying truth is you are a special creation by virtue of your salvation in Christ. Do you know you possess the raw power in your mouth to speak life and death to any condition or situation you find yourself in now or previously? In continuation of Luke 9:55, Jesus said," *the son of man did not come to destroy people's lives, but to save them*." Proverb 18:21 says Death and life are in the power of the tongue." Do you really understand this scripture? So how of life have you saved through the power in your tongue?

Another profound statement from the mouth of Jesus Christ is, "And from the days of John the Baptist until now the kingdom of heaven suffereth violence, and the violent taketh it by force." Yes, we are violent in the sense of using our mouth to decree according to the will of God; but are you violent in this regard? The purpose of this book, THERE'S FIRE IN YOUR MOUTH is to wake up the sleeping giant in you. The young adults are our main focus; this book wants you to reflect and remember your full strength in Christ.

As a young born-again child of God who has been saved by Jesus Christ, you are automatically equipped with the fullness of God in your body. 2Peter1:3 say, *"According as his divine power hath given unto us ALL THINGS that pertain unto life and godliness, through the knowledge of him that hath called us to glory and virtue."* You do not lack anything (weapons) with which to fight and win any battle of life because Ephesians 2:6 confirms that Christ hath raised us up together and made us sit together in heavenly places in Christ, *"far above principality, and power, and might, and dominion, and every name that is named, not only in this world, but also in that which is to come: and hath put all things under his feet, and gave him to be the head over all things to the church..."*-Eph 1:21,22.

This was the consciousness of Elijah, David, Moses, Samson, Gideon, Joshua, and many other great men of God of biblical times who conquered territories during their time. They all put their faith into action; they were violent because they knew within themselves that they carry the power of God, to trample upon the serpent and if they drink poison, it will not harm them (ref). This is the purpose of this book; here, we are trying to encourage you with what happened at Mount Carmel, where Elijah, God's only Prophet contested against 450 prophets of Baal and defeated them. Again, he was confronted by several troops of soldiers too, and defeated them also by a mere spoken word from his mouth.

Elijah's successor Elisha was also a man with absolute authority and power; with a curse from his mouth, forty-two (42) were killed by two she-bears who emerged from the nearby bush. There is power in your mouth; this book intends to encourage you to try your very best to recognize it now.

Finally, the place of prayer is very important; your attention is being drawn to the efficacy of prayer, without which nothing can be achieved. All biblical patriarchs were men of prayer; Samson was a man with the great power of God, but because he neglected prayer during his time, the great potential deposited in him became wasted. He could have done much more than he did during his lifetime as one of the judges in Israel. Maximum utilization of your God-given gifts coupled with a great prayer life can bring the expected successes into our lives, finances, businesses, families, and material well-being.

My prayer for the reader: may our good father in heaven, release great spiritual power and the gifts of the Holy

Spirit upon your head, to re-energize your ministerial, apostolic, and prophetic calling to fulfillment in the name of Jesus Christ, amen.

Chapter One: The Mount Carmel Experience.

- By evening it was Elijah's turn. He rebuilt the ruined altar of God that existed on Mount Carmel. He set the offering on top of the wood and then drenched the whole thing with water and prayed aloud: "LORD, the God of Abraham, Isaac, and Israel, let it be known today that you are God in Israel and that I am your servant and have done all these things at your command. Answer me, LORD, answer me, so these people will know that you, LORD, are God and that you are turning their hearts back again" (*1 Kings 18:36-37*).
- God answered with a spectacular display of fire from heaven, consuming the offering, licking up the sodden wood as well as every drop of water that had been poured over the altar. Even the rocks of the altar were consumed. The people fell on their faces, proclaiming, "The Lord, he is God; the Lord, he is God" (*1 Kings 18:39*). Elijah then ordered the people to execute the 850 false prophets according to the Mosaic Law (*Deuteronomy 13*).

Introduction

The Significance of Mount Carmel to The Christian

Rather than being a single mountain, Mount Carmel is actually a high, wooded mountain ridge. In the Bible, Mount Carmel is best known as the site of the prophet Elijah's dramatic showdown with 850 pagan prophets. *Carmel* means "vineyard," "orchard," or "garden" and reflects the fertile beauty of Mount Carmel's picturesque slopes. The mountainous ridge starts on the Mediterranean coast in the northwest part of Israel at the south shore of the Bay of Acre. From there, the range runs southeast down to the plain of Dothan. Running along the northeast side of the ridge is the Valley of Jezreel. At its highest point, Mount Carmel reaches over 1,700 feet above sea level.

Most notably, Mount Carmel is the scene of a spectacular head-to-head confrontation between the false prophets of Baal and Asherah and the One True God of Israel. The episode takes place during one of Israel's worst times of crisis under King Ahab. To please his wife, Jezebel, Ahab set up an altar to Baal at the top of Mount Carmel. Baal, the favorite deity of Jezebel, was reputed to be the god of rain and vegetation.

In *1 Kings 17:1–24,* Elijah the Tishbite enters the story as an emissary of the Lord. The prophet confronts Ahab and predicts a drought in response to Ahab and Jezebel's unholy devotion to Baal. When the end of the drought neared, to prove that the Lord God was the only true God, Elijah proposes a contest. All of Israel was summoned to Mount Carmel to witness the confrontation between Elijah and the false prophets of Baal and Asherah (1 Kings 18:19). The match would show whose god was able to send fire from heaven to consume their offerings. The prophets of Baal prayed all day and cut themselves violently to get Baal's attention, but no one answered (verses 28–29).

By evening it was Elijah's turn. He rebuilt the ruined altar of God that existed on Mount Carmel. He set the offering on top of the wood and then drenched the whole thing with water and prayed aloud: "LORD, the God of Abraham, Isaac, and Israel, let it be known today that you are God in Israel and that I am your servant and have done all these things at your command. Answer me, LORD, answer me, so these people will know that you, LORD, are God, and that you are turning their hearts back again" (*1 Kings 18:36–37*). God answered with a spectacular display of fire from heaven, consuming the offering, licking up the sodden wood as well as every drop of water that had been poured over the altar. Even the rocks of the altar were consumed. The people fell on their faces, proclaiming,

"The Lord, he is God; the Lord, he is God" (1 Kings 18:39). Elijah then ordered the people to execute the 850 false prophets according to the Mosaic Law (Deuteronomy 13). It seems that the prophet Elisha later used Mount Carmel as a home base (*2 Kings 4:25*). From ancient times, Mount Carmel has been regarded as a holy place and a symbol of beauty and fertility. In the tribal divisions, Mount Carmel was part of the territory of (western) Manasseh. Like the region of upper Galilee, Mount Carmel received plentiful rainfall in biblical times, producing lush, beautiful forests and rich grasslands on the lower slopes suitable for grazing. Isaiah associates God's glorious restoration of redeemed humanity with the *"splendor of Carmel"* (*Isaiah 35:2*). Solomon compares the head of his beloved with the beauty and nobility of Mount Carmel (*Song of Solomon 7:5).*

The Mount Carmel Challenge.

(Scripture Portion: 1 Kings 18: 17-40)

The Holy Spirit has certainly led the writer to give us a vivid and dramatic record of Elijah's great challenge on Mount Carmel. He is there in the presence of Ahab, the 450 prophets of Baal, 400 prophets of the groves, and a company of people from all of Israel. The question was: Is Baal the real God? Or is Jehovah the true God, and is Elijah His servant? No one present that day was left in any doubt as to the answer to these questions when *"the fire of the Lord fell..." ..."* (verse 38).

These biblical records are actual history, and in *1 Kings 18:17-40,* we read of fact, not fiction. The whole story is intensely dramatic. What a great God we have! Perhaps the most important value of the incident, however, is that it is permanently challenging. The lessons of the incident abide. What are they? Let us answer this question by asking: What is the greatest need in the Church today? Is it for men, money, machinery, or methods? No! What did Elijah need? *He needed evidence that God was alive and active;* so that the people would believe in Him and turn to Him –- now read verses 23-24 and 38-39. He needed fire, and that is what we need today –- fire, the symbol, evidence, and manifestation of God's presence and power

–- look up and compare Exodus 3:2; 13:21; 19:18; *Leviticus 9:24; 1 Chronicles 21:26; 2 Chronicles 7:1; Isaiah 4:4; Luke 3:16; Acts 2:3-4* and *Hebrews 12:29*. What we need is the burning, consuming, illuminating, and empowering *fire of the Holy Spirit* to fall upon the work that God has committed to us.

How can we obtain this fire? Verse 38 states – – "Then the fire of the Lord fell…"… what are the antecedents of this *"then"*? for it is clear that the fire of God only falls when all His requirements are met. *When* did it fall? In answering this we shall use an outline suggested by the late Canon Guy H. King.

It Was When the Altar Was Repaired

Verse 30. The very first thing Elijah did in preparation for the coming of the fire was to repair the altar of the Lord. Idolatry and apostasy had been prevalent for so long that God's altars had been broken down, and Elijah now engaged in the work of repair. What is the significance of this for us? Surely, the fire of the Lord only falls, (in the life, the church or the work that He has committed to us to do for Him), when the Lord is given His rightful place. Has the Lord His rightful place in your life and in all you are seeking to do in His name? –- look up *Colossians 1:18*.

Who is upon the throne -- the Lord Jesus or self? Who is first in your life -- a friend, a loved one or the Lord Himself?

It Was When the Sacrifice Was Offered

Verse 33. The sacrifice was a bullock, which Elijah cut up and placed, piece by piece, on the altar. Compare Romans 12:1 and 6:13, and ask yourself: How many of the pieces of my life have I really offered to the Lord upon the altar, and how many of my members are yielded fully to Him "as instruments of righteousness"? What about my hands, feet, eyes ears, lips, my home, job, pleasures, and friendships? Have I yielded all the "pieces" or" members" to Him?

It Was When the Water Was Poured

Verses 33-35. The pagan priests were notorious for their trickery in deceiving the people with false signs and lying wonders. Elijah was preparing to offset this, so after placing the pieces of sacrifice upon the altar he drenched both altar and sacrifice with water, not only once or twice but three times, until -- see verse 35! What things do we substitute for the fire of the Lord? Are we proud of our lovely churches, organs, choirs, dazzling oratory, good collections, etc.? What are any of these without the power of Pentecost?

It Was When the Prayer Was Made

Verses 36 and 37. Elijah was a man of prayer; it was the habit of his life. He did not only pray when he was in trouble -- look up *James 5:16-18*. Read verses 36 and 37 several times, and notice when, where and how he prayed. The one all-embracing condition which must be met if God's fire is to fall in -- prayer, more prayer, and yet more prayer. If we will *really* pray, sooner or later the fire will fall -- in our lives and in our work for the Lord.

The Testing That He Experienced

It has been suggested that there is a change in Elijah's praying between verses 36 and 37. In verse 36, Elijah prayed for the fire that all might know "" that *I* am your servant and have done all these things at your command""; but in verse 37 the change came. He prayed "" so these people will know that *you*, O Lord, are God and that *you* are turning their hearts back again."" Why do we want the fire of the Lord to fall, to be empowered for service and to be filled with the Holy Spirit? Do we want it for ourselves? It is only when our motive is that *God* should be glorified and *His Name* honored and exalted that the fire of the Lord will fall.

These are the prerequisites to Pentecost, to an outpouring of that consuming fire of the Holy Spirit. Let us pray that throughout our land and around the world the fire of the Lord may fall.

Closing Thought: Isaiah 4:3-5.

And it shall come to pass, that he that is left in Zion, and he that remaineth in Jerusalem, shall be called holy, even everyone that is written among the living in Jerusalem: When the Lord shall have washed away the filth of the daughters of Zion, and shall have purged the blood of Jerusalem from the midst thereof by the spirit of judgment, and by the spirit of burning. And the LORD will create upon every dwelling place of mount Zion, and upon her assemblies, a cloud and smoke by day, and the shining of a flaming fire by night: for upon all the glory shall be a defense.

LET THE FIRE FALL.

Let the fire fall prayer points tags: prayer points for fresh fire, prayer points for a fresh anointing, let the fire fall sermon, prayer for fire anointing, warfare prayer points with scriptures, prayer points for spiritual empowerment, prayer for a supernatural anointing for fresh fire, fresh fire from heaven, prayer points for holy spirit baptism, prayer points for prophetic anointing, fire for fire prayer, prayer points for power and authority, prayer points with scripture references.

Let The Fire Fall Prayer Points

Scripture Reading: 1 Kings 18:24

Let us begin our reflection with the Prayer to the Holy Spirit by St. Augustine:

"Breathe into me, Holy Spirit, that my thoughts may all be holy. Move-in me, Holy Spirit, that my work, too, maybe holy. Attract my heart, Holy Spirit, that I may love only what is holy. Strengthen me, Holy Spirit that I may defend all that is holy. Protect me, Holy Spirit, that I may always be holy".

Our scripture reference today recalls one of the most dramatic manifestations of God in the form of fire in the

Old Testament. Elijah's dramatic challenge grew out of his deep concern over the spiritual darkness that enveloped Israel the people of God. In a time like this when lukewarmness for the true God is on the increase, when there is a crisis of faith, the fire of divine love in many hearts getting cold, going to church is becoming boring, and many losing the joy of Christianity, lack of fruitfulness in the lives of many believers when there is great lack of divine evidence in the preaching of many believers when there is a great dryness in the heart of many professed believers when God or the faith no longer make sense to an increasing number of once baptized and confirmed Christians.

The grave need for the fresh outpouring of the Holy Spirit cannot be overstressed. At a time like this when the church is passing through a period of crisis when the preaching of many ministers is lacking in power to set hearts on fire, when ethnicity and divisions have crept into the Church and when believers' financial obligations have become more important to religious leaders of various hierarchies and ranks than the salvation of the believers' souls when it seems the Church is becoming more worldly, when many Christians are becoming more passive in their Christian commitments; such a time evidently reveals the extreme need for the FIRE of Pentecost. The absence of the Fire of Pentecost is responsible for the little impact believers are making in our world and government today. The first century Christians were able to convert their pagan world, because PENTECOST WAS A DAILY REALITY IN THEIR LIVES.

Hear Anthony de Mello, "The greatest need of Believers and the Church today is not new legislation, not new theology, not new structures, not new liturgies, not a new deal, but a new zeal; we need a fresh outpouring of the FIRE of Pentecost." At a time, such as this, we need the Elijahs of our time to rise up and pray the LORD to "SEND THE FIRE". Let us (members of the Daily Strength Family) together like the Apostles of old in obedience to Jesus earnestly and constantly pray during these nine days of Pentecost fasting and prayer to the Lord saying, "O LORD, SEND DOWN THE FIRE OF PENTECOST AGAIN IN OUR TIME". Child of God, as we prepare for this mighty outpouring of the FIRE of Pentecost, we must surrender our lives totally to the Lordship of Jesus Christ. Each one of us must invest a lot of time in earnest prayer of expectant faith to the Father to SEND THE FIRE. The Holy Spirit is given in answer to earnest prayer, so as we end today's reflection, make this song your earnest prayer: "Send down fire, Holy Ghost fire, Send down fire again, Holy Ghost fire."

Begin your prayer with this song: "Holy Ghost Fire, Fire fall on me, Holy......."

Lord Jesus, purge me of all sinfulness with the fire of the Holy Ghost in the name of Jesus. Come Holy Spirit, and fill the hearts of your faithful, and kindle in them the fire of Your Divine Love. Send forth Your Spirit and they shall be created, and You shall renew the face of the earth in the name of Jesus.

- Lord, set me on fire with the fire of the Holy Ghost, in the name of Jesus.
- Father your Spirit came and your Church was born, in wind and fire and words of power. Your Spirit came blowing fears aside, and in its place weak hearts were stronger. Your Spirit came as your word foretold, with dreams and signs, visions and wonders. Let your Spirit come on us as it was in the day of Pentecost, Renew our hearts which have grown cold with flames of Fire as on that Pentecost that this might be the Church that you desire in the name of Jesus. When the enemy deposit something in your body it brings you back. They can bring it through dreams. A satanic word can be deposited in a man's life. [Psa.9:6]. The heart of a man is deeper than a river. There are demons sent to

weaken a man during the time of prayer - **Gen 19: 23-29.**

- Father, you are the God that answereth by fire, let your fire fall upon the camp of the enemies manipulating my glory and destiny in the name of Jesus.
- Lord, let there be rain of fire upon my life that will destroy every deposit of Satan in my body.
- Lord, rain down fire from heaven into my family and let every wicked spirits die in the name of Jesus.
- Lord, let the rain of fire fall and destroy every evil plantation in my family in the name of Jesus.
- Father, send down your fire and destroy every altar of Satan taking decisions concerning my life in the name of Jesus.
- Lord, let the rain of fire go into my foundation and destroy every evil works that has been sown into my foundation in the name of Jesus.
- Lord, rain down your fire to destroy all the works of the devil in my life in the name of Jesus.
- Lord, let the household enemy be destroyed by fire in the name of Jesus.
- Lord, command your rain of fire to destroy any seed of the devil in my body in the name of Jesus.

- Let the smoke of fire cover the city of the wicked in the name of Jesus.

PROPHETIC DECLARATIONS

- Rain of fire will fall upon your enemies today.
- God will rain down fire on the city of the enemy today.
- Fire will consume every accusing finger pointing at you.
- Fire will consume anyone manipulating your life and ministry.
- By force by fire you will recover all.
- Fire will consume every deposit of the enemy in your life.
- Every satanic mark placed on you that makes people run away from you, fire will consume them.
- Every enemy tormenting you will be consumed by fire today.
- In the name above ever, let fire come down and destroy every satanic altar taking decision on you
- Let the fire of God consume every strongman in your life.
- Every deposit of the enemy in your body that is not allowing people to help you is destroyed by fire

- Fire of Holy Ghost will consume anyone sitting on your rights.
- Anyone diverting your blessings will be consumed by the fire of the Holy Ghost.
- As from now, the fire of God will work on your behalf.
- Whatever the Lord has not planted in your life that is causing problems for you is consumed by the fire of the Holy Ghost.

Prophecies For Today

- By 12pm this afternoon, something good will happen in your life.
- By 12pm this afternoon, fire will fall on the camp of your enemies.
- Any man or woman in the village that said no good news will be heard about you, by 12pm God will consume them by fire.

LESSONS AT MOUNT CARMEL"

Introduction

Observing God's interaction with Elijah and Elijah's spiritual journey in his day provides insight and principles for us in our day which is not unlike what Elijah faced. The transitions in Elijah's life follow a definite instruction from the Lord. "And the word of the Lord came to Elijah"

There is much to learn from Elijah. So far, some key elements of Elijah's life are his bold prayer, his listening ear, his prompt obedience, and his contentment to serve wherever God put him.

- Lessons from the Palace where Elijah boldly announced God's judgment for sin. 1 Kings 17:1
- Lessons from the brook where Elijah learned to trust God in obscurity and isolation. 17:2-7
- Lessons from Zarephath where Elijah learned to trust God in ministry 17:8-24
- Lessons from the Palace Part two where Elijah confronted Ahab again Kings 18:1-19

You Need the Fire In Your Mouth? Hear This!

- God's assignments are not always comfortable but critical.
- God strategically places His "agents" everywhere.
- God connects resources along the way of obedience.
- Only a renewed awareness of God's perspective and presence can overcome
- Tough assignments are not punishment for sin.
- God is perfectly able to protect His children.
- Much of the troubles in our life are the result of our rebellion.
- God often calls on us to boldly confront evil and speak truth.

Lessons from Mount Carmel where Elijah confronted Baalism 18:20-41

So Ahab sent a message among all the sons of Israel and brought the prophets together at Mount Carmel. And Elijah came near to all the people and said, "How long will you hesitate between two opinions? If the Lord is God, follow Him; but if Baal, follow him." But the people did not answer him a word. 18:20-21

Everyone gathered at Mount Carmel by the king's command. The distance to Mount Carmel from Samaria is

57 miles, about a good day's walk. Mount Carmel rises up to a height of 1,791 feet from a 24-mile-long mountain range along coast.

God will not share loyalty with anyone. We must serve one or the other. We can't have it both ways. Some think we have three options.

- Follow God and God alone.
- Follow the World and the world alone.
- Embrace the best aspects of Christianity and the world.

God unequivocally declares that we must choose one or the other. To choose a mediating position is to choose against God. The response of the people is disheartening. Rather than choose one or the other, they refused to make a choice. The word here means to "skip", hesitate, and be lame. They refused to commit one way or the other.

B. Elijah challenged the false prophets of Baal

Then Elijah said to the people, "I alone am left a prophet of the Lord, but Baal's prophets are 450 men. Now let them give us two oxen, and let them choose one ox for themselves and cut it up, and place it on the wood, but put no fire under it, and I will prepare the other ox, and lay it on the wood, and I will not put a fire under it. Then you call on the name of your god, and I will call on the name of the Lord, and the God who answers by fire, He is God." And all the people answered and said, "That is a good idea."

Life is full of choices. At times I just hate making another choice in the day. Americans are super spoiled with the number of choices we have available. Some choices are insignificant, other choices have the potential of effecting the course and direction of the rest of our life. Today, we track Elijah up Mount Carmel where he solicits a significant choice from the people of Israel and provides a very powerful incentive to make the right one. The people of Israel had readily embraced the shallow sensual gratification of Baalism over the internal spiritual obedience to Yahweh which held the promise of both temporal and eternal blessing. Every time the people shifted their focus from the eternal God to some devil-designed power, they plunged into sensual and sexual addiction. Elijah nursed a compelling drive and passion to eliminate this destructive evil influence on the people of God.

The people gathered on Mount Carmel, thought to be a sacred site of Baal worship who was supposed to bring fertility to his worshippers, he issued a clear challenge to the people. It is interesting the prominence of mountain top experiences.

Chapter Two: The Captains of Fifty Experience

- When the first Captain told Elijah, "O man of God, the king says, 'Come down,'' it was not a request from a King to a prophet of God, it was an act of disdain for the authority of the God of Israel. Elijah confirms this by calling for God's judgment:
- "If I am a man of God, let fire come down from heaven and consume you and your fifty." Then fire came down from heaven and consumed him and his fifty.

Introduction

Another tumultuous incident in the bible in which fire fell from heaven and consumed its target by a command of a person through the use of mouth was the story of the three (3) captains of fifty soldiers. This story is recorded in *2 Kings 1*, where we find Elijah's encounter with King Ahaziah and his three Captains of Fifty. Ahaziah was crippled by recent injuries and sent men to consult a pagan god. Elijah intercepted his messengers and sent them back with a question and a judgment: "Is it because there is no God in Israel that you are going off to consult Baal-Zebub, the god of Ekron? Therefore, this is what the Lord says: 'You will not leave the bed you are lying on.

You will certainly die!" So, Ahaziah sent for Elijah to be brought to him. At the end of this story 103 people are dead. Verse 15 indicates the gravity of the situation – from beginning to end – for Elijah: "The angel of the LORD said to Elijah, "Go down with him; do not be afraid of him." So he arose and went down with him to the king." Until the angel of the Lord told him to go, certain death awaited Elijah at the hands of King Ahaziah. The Captains and their men were sent to march a 'Prophet of God' to his death. They knew who and what he was. No one concerned was an unsuspecting soldier 'just carrying out orders.' When the first Captain told Elijah, "O man of God, the king says,

'Come down," it was not a request from a King to a prophet of God, it was an act of disdain for the authority of the God of Israel. Elijah confirms this by calling for God's judgment: "If I am a man of God, let fire come down from heaven and consume you and your fifty." Then fire came down from heaven and consumed him and his fifty" The second Captain of Fifty ignored the obvious, said the same thing, and suffered the same fate; fire from God consumed them, too. The third Captain had sense enough to believe the obvious. He fell on his knees and begged for his life and those of his men. He had worked out that which King Ahaziah refused to acknowledge: That there was indeed a God in Israel! All they had to do was ask.

The power which Elijah exercised here, is based on the authority Jesus has extended to us; we are using the same authority with Him. Thus, everything Jesus utters is in our name, and everything we utter is in His name. He doesn't make a decision without us, and we don't make a decision without Him. This is hugely profound! Elijah always heard from heaven.

We are jointly seated with Him in heavenly places (*Eph 2:6*) far above all principality and power, and might, and dominion, and every name, not only in this world but also in that which is to come (1:21). It has been decided from heaven. We are Chris's legal representatives on earth.

What we say in the earth is endorsed in the heavens. Understanding this is very important. It means you alone a can take a stand on God's word and effect a change on the basis of this understanding, and it will be endorsed from heaven. This is the profound understanding Elijah had that made fire blaze to trail him.

Some people think that until all the Christian in the world come together to stand against Satan and his antics and deception, then nothing can change. Every Christian is not at the same level of faith or knowledge at every point in time then; neither are they now, however, what God expects is that those of us who have come to maturity, who have an understanding of His word and of the times, will take our stand and our place in Christ to keep Satan under our feet where he belongs. That is what is important; and that was what Elijah did at his time, which you must do today. Let the fire come from your mouth to consume the enemy.

With this kind of knowledge, you maintain control of things in your life, your environment, and the world. You nullify Satan's plans and works and pull them down by the power of the living Christ. Don't be troubled by what is happening in the world today; use your authority in Christ. You reign in Him and through Him over Satan, darkness, the world and circumstances. Therefore, subdue your world. Let nothing but Christ reign in your physical body, in your job or business, in your family, and your world. Remember, you are seated with Him in glory, with the same authority. This is the secret; most immature Christians have not come to terms with this reality.

Judgment Of Sin and Wickedness

(2 KINGS 1)

REWARD FOR SIN: Ahaziah's injury; SEEKS BAAL-ZEBUB

Moab rebelled against Israel after the death of Ahab. Now Ahaziah fell through the lattice of his upper room in Samaria, and was injured; so he sent messengers and said to them, "Go, inquire of Baal-Zebub, the god of Ekron, whether I shall recover from this injury."

a. **Moab rebelled against Israel after the death of Ahab**: The reign of Ahab was a spiritual disaster for the Northern Kingdom, but it was a time of political security and economic prosperity. After his death, the kingdom of Moab found a good opportunity to remove their nation from the domination of Israel.

i. "Their land was immediately east of the Dead Sea and shared an indefinite border with Israel to the north at approximately the point where the Jordan River enters the Dead Sea." (Dilday)

ii. Moab had been under Israelite domination since the days of David (2 Samuel 8:2 and 8:11-12). This rebellion of Moab in the days of Ahaziah was a sign of the decline of Israel's power and of the judgment of God as a result of sins and wickedness.

b. **Ahaziah fell through the lattice of his upper room in Samaria**: This was surely an unexpected crisis. Such accidents happen to kings and peasants both.

i. "The king apparently leaned against the wooden screen and fell through from the second-floor balcony to the ground below." (Dilday)

c. **Go, inquire of Baal-Zebub, the god of Ekron, whether I shall recover from this injury**: Ahaziah showed that he was a true worshipper of the pagan god Baal-Zebub because he turned to this god in his time of trouble.

i. "This could suggest that Baal-Zebub was a god who warded off plagues that were brought on by flies. There are numerous references to 'fly gods' in classical literature." (Dilday)

ii. "He was the local god of Ekron, and probably was used at first to drive away flies. Afterwards, he became a very respectable devil, and was supposed to have great power and influence. In the New Testament, Beelzebub is a common name for Satan himself, or the prince of devils." (Adam Clarke)

iii. "Men love the gods that are most like unto themselves, so it is not surprising to see Ahaziah sending to this miserable Philistine god." (Knapp)

Speak Up Against Sin And Evil - *(3-4) Elijah's message to Ahaziah for his unbelief.*

But the angel of the LORD said to Elijah the Tishbite, "Arise, go up to meet the messengers of the king of Samaria, and say to them, 'Is it because there is no God in Israel that you are going to inquire of Baal-Zebub, the god of Ekron?' Now therefore, thus says the LORD: 'You shall not come down from the bed to which you have gone up, but you shall surely die.'" So Elijah departed.

a. **Is it because there is no God in Israel**: There is little doubt that King Ahaziah believed that Yahweh lived, but he *lived* as if there were no God in Israel. He was a practical atheist, and the way he sought Baal-Zebub *instead* of the LORD demonstrated this.

b. **You shall not come down from the bed to which you have gone up, but you shall surely die**: Ahaziah did not seek help from the real God; therefore he will get no

real help. Instead, this will be an occasion for the real God to send a message of judgment to King Ahaziah.
i. According to Wiseman, when ancients sought their gods about medical issues, "The result was usually given in medical prognostic texts as 'he will live/die' as in verses 6, 16 (*you will certainly die*)." This means that Elijah's words **but you shall surely die** were phrased as a medical diagnosis. It was as if Elijah said, "Here's your diagnosis, Ahaziah: Your condition is fatal and irreversible."

ii. In fact, this was a *mercy* to Ahaziah. God told him something that few people know. His death was imminent, and he had time to repent and prepare to meet God.

iii. This prophetic announcement might also explain why Ahaziah did not want to seek an answer from the LORD: He knew what the answer would be. In seeking Baal-Zebub for an answer, Ahaziah may have wanted to find a god to tell him what he wanted to hear.

Trade Mark Of A True Man Of God: - **(5-8) the prophet asked the messengers to return to Ahaziah.**

And when the messengers returned to him, he said to them, "Why have you come back?" So they said to him, "A man came up to meet us, and said to us, 'go, return to the king who sent you, and says to him, "Thus says the LORD:

'*Is it* because *there is* no God in Israel *that* you are sending to inquire of Baal-Zebub, the god of Ekron? Therefore you shall not come down from the bed to which you have gone up, but you shall surely die.'"'" Then he said to them, "What kind of man *was it* who came up to meet you and told you these words?" So they answered him, "A hairy man wearing a leather belt around his waist." And he said, "It *is* Elijah the Tishbite."

a. **A man came up to meet us**: Though they were sent to seek a word from the pagan priests of Baal-Zebub, the word from Elijah persuaded them so much that they didn't follow through on their original mission.

i. "This official delegation from the king would certainly not have turned back from their royal assignment just because some anonymous wayfarer asked them to. There must have been an irresistible quality to Elijah's personality, a forceful spiritual presence, which compelled them to obey this stranger even though they didn't know who he was." (Dilday)

b. **What kind of man was it who came up to meet you**: Ahaziah clearly suspected it was the Prophet Elijah who spoke this word. His suspicion was confirmed when the man was described as a hairy man wearing a leather belt around his waist.

i. The Hebrew words translated hairy man literally mean, "possessor of hair." "This description more than likely refers to the hairy animal skins he wore clinched around his waist with a leather belt." (Dilday)

ii. Identifying Elijah by his clothes also connected him to the ministry of John the Baptist, who dressed in hairy skins from animals (Matthew 3:4). When the priests and Levites saw him they asked, "Are you Elijah?" (John 1:19-21)

iii. "Either because Elijah had much hair on his head and face, or because, as a prophet, he wore a rough garment (Zechariah 13:4), as a pattern of repentance." (Trapp)

Punishment For Disobedience: - (9-10).Elijah appears before Ahaziah to confirm the God judgment

Then the king sent to him a captain of fifty with his fifty men. So he went up to him; and there he was, sitting on the top of a hill. And he spoke to him: "Man of God, the king has said, 'come down!'" So Elijah answered and said to the captain of fifty, "If I *am* a man of God, then let fire come down from heaven and consume you and your fifty men." And fire came down from heaven and consumed him and his fifty.

a. **The king sent to him a captain of fifty with his fifty men**: This should have been plenty of men to capture one prophet. Clearly, Ahaziah sent *more* men than were normally required.

b. **Man of God, the king has said, "Come down":** The captain here admitted the righteousness of Elijah when he called him "**Man of God**." Therefore they were wrong in doing this, even though they were on orders from their king.

i. The Bible clearly teaches that we owe submission to the government and governing authorities (*Romans 13:1-2*). Yet in the human sphere, the Biblical command to submit is never absolute, but always conditioned by the greater responsibility to submit to God (*Acts 5:29*). This commander should have resisted the ungodly and immoral command from King Ahaziah and obeyed God instead. His fifty men should have refused to obey the ungodly and immoral command of their captain.

c. **If I am a man of God, then let fire come down from heaven**: Elijah put the issue in stark contrast. If he really were a man of God, then the captain and his men were on an ungodly and immoral mission. Since Elijah could not bring down fire from heaven without Divine approval, he asked *God* to evaluate these men and the rightness of their actions against God's prophet.

i. "Either they did not hold him to be a prophet, or they gloried in putting the power of their master above that of Jehovah. In any case, the insult was less against Elijah than Elijah's God." (Meyer)

ii. Elijah did not say, "You bet I am a man of God." Instead, he answered If I am a man of God. Essentially Elijah said, "You say I am a man of God even though you are not acting like it. Maybe I am and maybe I am not. Let's let God decide by fire."

iii. "Some have blamed the prophet for destroying these men, by bringing down fire from heaven upon them. But they do not consider that it was no more possible for *Elijah* to bring down fire from heaven, than for *them* to do it. *God alone* could send the fire; and as he is *just* and *good*, he would not have destroyed these men had there not been a *sufficient cause* to justify the act." (Clarke)

d. **Fire came down from heaven and consumed him and his fifty**: God brought judgment on these men who acted as if Yahweh was not a real God and as if Elijah was not truly His servant.

i. The captain commanded Elijah to "Come down!" The man of God didn't come down, but the fire of God did.

ii. "It must be noted that the demands made of Elijah were wrong. A king had no right to ask such allegiance and his actions should always be subordinate to God's word. God was protecting his word and his servant." (Wiseman).

Demonstration Of Power: - **(11-12) Judgment also comes upon a second captain.**

Then he sent to him another captain of fifty with his fifty men. And he answered and said to him: "Man of God thus has the king said, 'Come down quickly!' " So Elijah answered and said to them, "If I *am* a man of God, let fire come down from heaven and consume you and your fifty men." And the fire of God came down from heaven and consumed him and his fifty.

a. **Man of God, thus has the king said**: The second captain repeated the same error as the first captain, but with even more guilt because he knew what happened to the first captain. The judgment upon the first group should have warned this second captain and his fifty men.

i. The specific request of the second captain (Come down quickly!) shows that the second captain made his request even *more* bold and demanding.

ii. The people and leaders of Israel had gone after pagan gods so long that they could not distinguish between the imaginary, impotent gods of the pagan world and Yahweh, the LORD God of Israel. They thought that Yahweh was just as powerless as their own useless gods.

b. **If I am a man of God, let fire come down from heaven and consume you and your fifty men**: Elijah left the matter in God's hands, and God again responded in dramatic judgment.

The Importance of Humility: **(13-15): the third captain saved by humility and obedience.**

Again, he sent a third captain of fifty with his fifty men. And the third captain of fifty went up, and came and fell on his knees before Elijah, and pleaded with him, and said to him: "Man of God, please let my life and the life of these fifty servants of yours be precious in your sight. Look, fire has come down from heaven and burned up the first two captains of fifties with their fifties. But let my life now be precious in your sight." And the angel of the LORD said to Elijah, "Go down with him; do not be afraid of him." So he arose and went down with him to the king.

a. **Fell on his knees before Elijah, and pleaded with him**: The third captain approached his mission in a completely different manner. He came to Elijah humbly, recognizing that he really was a Man of God. Perhaps the third captain looked at the two blackened spots of scorched earth nearby before he spoke to Elijah.

b. **Go down with him; do not be afraid of him**: It wasn't that God did not want Elijah to go to King Ahaziah; it was that Ahaziah, his captains, and their soldiers all acted as if there were no God in Israel. When the request was made wisely and humbly, Elijah went.

i. There were many reasons why Ahaziah wanted to arrest Elijah, even though he already heard the prophecy through Elijah. Perhaps he wanted Elijah to reverse his word of doom and would use force to compel him to do it. Perhaps he just wanted to show his rage against this prophet who had troubled him and his father Ahab for so long. Perhaps he wanted to dramatically silence Elijah to discourage future prophets from speaking boldly against the king of Israel. God assured Elijah that he had nothing to fear from Ahaziah.

Consistency And Fearlessness:- (16) Elijah delivers the same message to Ahaziah.

Then he said to him, "Thus says the LORD: 'Because you have sent messengers to inquire of Baal-Zebub, the god of Ekron, *is it* because *there is* no God in Israel to inquire of His word? Therefore you shall not come down from the bed to which you have gone up, but you shall surely die.'"

a. Is it because there is no God in Israel to inquire of His word: This was the same message Elijah gave to the men Ahaziah sent to inquire of Baal-Zebub. The message from God did not change just because Ahaziah didn't want to hear it the first time.

5. (17-18) Ahaziah dies and leaves no successor.

So *Ahaziah* died according to the word of the LORD which Elijah had spoken. Because he had no son, Jehoram became king in his place, in the second year of Jehoram the son of Jehoshaphat, king of Judah. Now the rest of the acts of Ahaziah which he did, *are* they not written in the book of the chronicles of the kings of Israel?

a. So Ahaziah died according to the word of the LORD which Elijah had spoken: The proof was in the result. Elijah was demonstrated to be a man of God because his prophecy was fulfilled just as spoken. Ahaziah did not recover from his fall through the lattice.

i. "Everything he did was weak, faithless, and miserable; he achieved nothing but ruin and failure. He let Moab rebel. He hurt himself in a clumsy accident. He foolishly attempted to use military force against Elijah. And worse, he sought help in the wrong place – in Philistia at the altar of a pagan god." (Dilday)

Chapter Three: Elisha and The Two Bears Experience.

This seems harsh, but God and His leaders have, on occasion, acted harshly in order to impress upon man the seriousness of life and the Word of God. Ananias and Saphira are an illustration of this in the New Testament.

James 3:6 says, "And the tongue is a fire..." Fire plays two major roles; firstly, it burns to destroy, and secondly, it burns to refine (remove unwanted material deposits). At the time of Elijah, Elisha, and others, it was used to destroy every evil that stands on God's way; but today, grace has replaced the old order.

Introduction

In this chapter, we shall be talking about the power in your tongue; the power of life and death, blessing and cursing. You do not need anointing or the power of God before you can place a curse, but certainly, you need anointing from on high to effect special blessings on anyone. Elisha, our example here, had just performed a miracle – healed Jericho's water. A man with such enormous power could have released blessings upon these forty-two (42) lads, but instead released a curse upon them which led to being torn- apart from by two female bears.

James 3:6 says, "And the tongue is a fire..." Fire plays two major roles; firstly, it burns to destroy, and secondly, it burns to refine (remove unwanted material deposits). At the time of Elijah, Elisha, and others, it was used to destroy every evil that stands in God's way; but today, grace has replaced the old order. Fire is used by knowledgeable and matured believers to stand against Satan and his cohorts on the one hand, and on the other hand, it is used to destroy demonic deposits and set free (deliver) Satan's captives.

Why Did Elisha Kill the Children?

In 2 Kings 2, Elisha is confronted by a group of children mocking him, so he killed them. His response seems so excessive. Why didn't he forgive or just ignore them?

First, the Hebrew word translated "children" (or young lads in the NASB) refers to men who were in their youth, so typically this meant men between the ages of 18 and 30. Most modern translations use the word "youth" in this passage, not children, to reflect that this mob was not a mere group of children teasing an old man. These were young men who knew exactly who they were mocking and what they were doing. So, we must consider the context of these events to understand why they mocked Elisha and why Elisha responded with a curse.

2Kings 2:23 Then he went up from there to Bethel; and as he was going up by the way, young lads came out from the city and mocked him and said to him, "Go up, you baldhead; go up, you baldhead!" 2Kings 2:24 When he looked behind him and saw them, he cursed them in the name of the lord. And there came forth two she bears out of the wood, and tare forty-two of them.

These men are in the same area in which all these events take place, so it is clear they understood what had just happened to Elijah. Notice their chant to Elisha: "Go up, bald head, go up..." That phrase means they wished Elisha would disappear up in the clouds just as Elijah had gone up earlier. Their chant reveals their hearts. They do not wish to bear the chastisement of a prophet of God. Their sin convicts them, and they want to cast off the restraints of God's word delivered through the prophets. They were pleased to see Elijah go, and now they wish to see Elisha gone as well.

So these youths were no innocent group of children. They were a large gang of 40+ men, who surrounded Elisha mocking and probably threatening him. More importantly, they demonstrated their unbelieving and blasphemous hearts in the way they treated the anointed prophet of God. Therefore, Elisha acted under the influence of the Spirit to speak a curse against these men and their wicked ways.

Fulfilling Elisha's prophecy, the Lord sent two bears to attack the men. Elisha walked away unharmed, yet the forty-two men did not. Also note the Bible says the youth were torn apart, which means gravely harmed but not necessarily killed (though some may have died). This was the Lord's judgment on these men, not merely Elisha's. Elisha didn't control the actions of the bear, but we know God did.

This moment was orchestrated by the Lord to ensure the people of Israel understood that Elisha would have the same power God gave to Elijah in his day. In fact, Elisha performed twice as many miracles over his tenure as did Elijah. There was fire in his mouth.

We must remember, also, that the Word of God, which is alive and active, is also the mighty channel the Spirit of God uses to bring men out of darkness to faith in Jesus Christ and to change them by making them like His Son. As a light that shines in the darkness of this world it exposes man's sin, but man loves the darkness because it hides his evil deeds. He hates the light for that very reason; it exposes his evil deeds (cf. John 3:19-21). These may be deeds of ignorance, of apathy, or of out-and-out rebellion or a combination, but regardless, it often results in hatred of the light that is manifest in one form or another.

The gospel, which is contained in the Word of God, is the power of God unto salvation. Satan, of course, who holds people in bondage to death, neither wants people saved nor experiencing the power of a Christ-changed life by the power of the Spirit. For this reason, as the adversary, Satan never gets busier than when the Word of God begins to be proclaimed and taught. He hates the Word and people of the Word, especially those engaged in its proclamation. They become the target for his attacks in whatever form he can muster.

Therefore, Bible teaching ministries, pastors, teacher, and other believers involved in the ministry of the Word can expect opposition. It simply goes with the territory. This is clearly evident in this short passage before us. In fact, this is one of the key lessons of these few verses. This was true with Moses, Elijah, and with all the prophets. We can expect attack from the world which lies under the control of Satan. But isn't it sad when attack comes from the people of God themselves? Unfortunately, Satan is able to use God's own people to hinder the Word, as he did with the children of Israel on many occasions.

Our Lord said, "O Jerusalem, Jerusalem, who kills the prophets and stones those who are sent to her" (Matt. 23:37). Not all Israel was true spiritual Israel, but the fact still remains true. Satan is often able to establish a beachhead among the saints.

Elisha Heads For Bethel (2:23a)

Following the ministry in Jericho (which portrayed a kind of first fruits of the land) Elisha, as a man of God under the direction of God and with the Word of God moves on into the land to minister to the people. They were a people living in idolatry and badly in need of the Word.

"Bethel" means "house of God" or "place of God." This name spoke of worship and fellowship with God. There was also a school of the prophets in Bethel, but in spite of this the city was now idolatrous and anything but a center of worship. Hosea, who ministered after Elisha, called this city *Bethaven* "house of wickedness" a name of shame (cf. Hos. 4:15; 5:8; 10:5). It was so-called by Hosea because of the idolatrous worship Jeroboam had established in order to effect a complete separation between Israel and Judah. Out of his greed for power and his fear that if Israel went back to Jerusalem to worship, he established two new places of worship in the north with golden calves as the symbol of worship: one at Bethel and the other at Dan. This was of course in complete disobedience to the directives of the Old Testament Scripture.

"*Beth*" means "house and "*el*" means God. *Aven* is the Hebrew *awen* which means "trouble, sorrow, idolatry, wickedness, and emptiness." The word *awen* seems to have two primary facets to its meaning: (a) it portrays an iniquity that causes sorrow, calamity, and failure (Prov. 22:8). (b) But it also portrays an emptiness that moves on to idolatry as a human means of filling the emptiness. The point is when men are empty of God and His Word; they will fill their lives with vain things whether material or philosophic. This leads to idolatry, which leads to iniquity, which leads to calamity.

Bethel needed the Word to show them their sin and to bring them back to the Lord. This was their only hope and Satan was active to stop it. Elisha was undoubtedly able to minister to the needs of certain ones there (the remnant), but the city as a whole never really turned to the Lord and His Word. Satan was well entrenched there. This is another fact we sometimes have to face. And when this is the case we may need to simply move on as Elisha did and as Paul and others did.

"And as he was going . . ." calls our attention to the time of the attack. It occurred simply in the normal process of his travels to the city. We never know (though the Lord does) when Satan or others under his control or influence, are going to attack. Just about the time, we might think pressures are easing up, and things are getting better--the attack increases. This is why we must always, in spite of how things appear, take heed lest we fall (1 Cor 10:12); why we must look to ourselves lest we be tempted (Gal 6:1); and why we must be careful how we are walking (Eph 5:15) because we live in an evil world and Satan is on the prowl. He is warring against the saints.

Elisha Is Mocked (2:23b)

"Young lads." The KJV has "little children" which really misses the meaning here. These were not children, but young men. The word "lads" is the Hebrew *naar* and was used by servants, soldiers, and of Isaac when he was 28 years old. This was a crowd of young men, perhaps students of the false prophets, who were here as antagonists to Elisha's prophetic ministry and authority. If not students, they were sent by the false prophets or idolatrous priests of Bethel to stop Elisha from entering the city. In Elisha, Satan had an enemy and he was acting to protect his territory. Remember, however, Elisha was going to Bethel not to curse, but to bless.

"Came out of the city and mocked him . . . Go up, you baldhead." "Mocked" is the Hebrew *galas* and denotes a scornful belittling of something or someone, but it issues from an attitude that counts as valuelessness that which is really of great value.

Leaders have always had to deal with disrespect. It is seen throughout the Old Testament and it is found in the New Testament as well. But the greatest disrespect here is in relation to God. These young men, undoubtedly under Satan's influence, were attacking not just Elisha, the man, but they were also attacking his message. But the issue was, regardless of the personality of the man, his physical appearance, or even his shortcomings, Elisha was God's man with God's message. As a result, in the final analysis they were mocking or rejecting God and what He was attempting to do through Elisha as God's spokesman. Elisha was simply an instrument of God (cf. 2 Thess. 5:12, 13 "on account of the work"). The work referred to in 1 Thessalonians is God's work--the work of building men in the Word and in Christ through these men. And there is a certain sense in which this applies to all believers.

The attack of these young men is twofold:

(1) "Go up"… "go up." That is, ascend up as you claim Elijah did. The translation of Elijah was a miracle of God and portrayed the biblical truth and hope of the translation of the saints. Though Old Testament saints did not understand this, it was still a type of this truth. Elisha was a prophet of God and by doing this these young men were denying the work of God, denying the Word of God and God's actions in history.

(2) The second aspect of the attack is seen in the words: "you baldhead." Whether Elisha was actually bald, or whether he had a different hairstyle, i.e., cropped short on top, they were ridiculing the prophet and telling him to get lost like Elijah. Krummacher writes:

Baldness was regarded by the lower orders as a kind of disgrace; for as it was one of the usual consequences of leprosy, so it was accounted a sign of personal and mental degradation. Hence, in using this opprobrious epithet, the young profligates had a most malicious intention. Their expressions are not to be viewed as a mere burst of youthful wantonness; but as poisoned arrows, pointed and directed by refined and satanic malignity. It is as if they had said, "Thou effeminate leper! Thou would-be prophet! We fear thee not! Go up! Go up!" as if they mean, "Imitate thy master!" . . . It seems to have been a scoffing allusion to the ascent of Elijah; partly skeptical, and partly in derision of Elisha.

These attacks are typical of the schemes and methods by which Satan seeks to nullify the ministry of God's saints and the work of God. He attacks the message (the Word) and the messenger or both. He seeks to discourage or discredit the teacher or he attacks those hearing the message. Regarding the messenger, Satan may seek to call attention to petty issues, circumstances, misunderstandings, or focus on personalities, or physical appearance. It can be almost anything, but whatever, it is a means to a beachhead from whence he seeks to launch one attack after another to get people's eyes off the Lord and their ears closed to His Word. We must be careful that we do not cooperate with Satan and throw fuel on his fires.

The important thing here is Elisha's reaction to this and God's action in response. This is designed to emphasize to us the seriousness of the issues here.

Elisha Curses the Young Men (2:24a)

This seems harsh, but God and His leaders have, on occasion, acted harshly in order to impress upon man the seriousness of life and the Word of God. Ananias and Saphira are an illustration of this in the New Testament.

(1) What Elisha did not do: Before looking at what Elisha did, let's consider for a moment what he did not do! (a) He did not turn and run. (b) He did not argue with them or run after them (Matt 7:6). (c) He did not compromise his message. (d) He was not acting or reacting out of self love or anxiety or self-defense from the standpoint of his ego or pride. (e) He did not complain to the Lord or want to throw in the towel. (f) He simply ignored their words, actions, and attitudes. God's response proves this.

What does this teach us? When trouble strikes, we should never resort to the solutions of the world, i.e., to human viewpoint escape or defense tactics (cf. Ps. 143:11-12; 147:10-11).

(2) What Elisha did: Elisha took up his armor, "He cursed them in the name of the Lord." This is not cursing for cursing or reviling for reviling (1 Pet. 2:23). He was trusting in the Lord and leaving it in God's hands. The key here is in the word "curse." It does not mean to swear with vile words. This is the Hebrew word *galal* meaning "be swift, slight, trifling, or of little account." The primary meaning is "to be light or slight." Both verb and noun forms seem to represent a formula that expresses a removal or lowering from the place of blessing.

Cursing stands in contrast to the word blessing or favor (cf. Gen. 27:11, 12). The emphasis is on the absence, reversal, or removal of a blessed state or rightful position which brings God's protection, provision, and blessing. The principle is very simple: without God's blessed salvation and protection, we all stand cursed. The moment God removed His wall of protection from Job, Satan attacked him and wreaked havoc in Job's life.

So Elisha, as a prophet, saw their hardened and rebellious condition, unresponsive to correction. In the name of the Lord (i.e. by His authority) Elisha simply turned them over to the Lord and to their own devices, which had the effect of removing them from even the common protection of

God. He probably said something like, "may God deal with you according to what you deserve," or "may you be cursed for your sins of rebellion." This would demonstrate to the city and to people all around a vital truth: without the Lord, there is no protection and that blasphemy of God's servants and His Word in order to hinder God's message is serious business. Note that Elisha did not call out the bears, God did. Two female bears (not three bears--papa bear, mamma bear, and baby bear) came out and tore up forty-two young men.

You would think this would strike the fear of God into the hearts of the entire area for years to come. But no--the heart of man is such that they either ignore it, reject it, or soon forget it.

Conclusion

God does not take it lightly when we ignore His Word or hinder its propagation in the world among His people. This is serious business (cf. *1 Cor 3:16-17* with *10; 11:30*).

As believers, we should expect opposition. The more we move out for the Lord, the more attacks we may have to face from our adversary through his various schemes (cf. *1 Pet 4:10-12*). As Paul stated in *2 Timothy 3:12*, "In fact, everyone who wants to live a godly life in Christ Jesus will be persecuted" (NIV).

We need more Elisha, those who will stand fast and act in biblical ways leaving the results to the Lord. This is precisely what Paul did in connection with the strong criticism often leveled at him by some of the Corinthians (cf. 1 Cor. 4:1f). As with Elisha and Paul, we need to move forward in our ministries while always trusting God to make a way and remove the obstacles.

Chapter Four: The Place Of Prayer.

- When you need personal revival.
- When you need fresh fire for fighting the battles of life.
- When you need the power of the Holy Spirit to enable fulfill your destiny in life.

Introduction.

Reasons Why We Pray.

In the Bible, God commands people, multiple times, to pray. But why do we need to pray? This is a question many Christians, as well as people with other beliefs, have asked. If God is in control of human history and also directs individual lives, what's the point of praying? The answer lies in understanding what prayer is. If you see prayer merely as a means of taking some level of control of your life and the world — as a means of leverage — then you will inevitably be troubled by what appears to be unanswered prayer. But if you see prayer primarily as an ongoing conversation with God, then you'll realize there is really no such thing as an unanswered prayer.

If prayer is first and foremost a conversation between you and God, then His promise to always listen may be the answer your heart needs most.

God might not choose to do what you ask Him to do when you ask Him to do it. You might have seasons when you find it hard to hear what He's saying for all sorts of reasons. It's hard when someone says no, or even not yet, to what seems like a good and valid request. But if prayer is first and foremost a conversation between you and God, then His promise to always listen may be the answer your heart needs most. There is a famous verse in the Bible that is often misinterpreted, and it's vital to the questions we're thinking about here: "Take delight in the LORD, and He will give you the desires of your heart" (*Psalm 37:4*, N I V).

You can interpret this verse as saying if you focus on enjoying God, He will give you whatever you want. Or you can understand it to mean that if you take delight in God, over and above anything else in your life, He will shape your heart so it wants the things He already wants to give you. His desires will become your desires. It's safe to say that the second interpretation is more consistent with the teaching of the rest of the Bible. Scripture does not guarantee God will provide you whatever you want right now. With this in mind, let's look at the reasons we choose to pray — and some reasons we often choose not to.

1'specific Sections of Content.

- Why Pray If God Already Knows What Will Happen?
- Why Pray If God Already Knows What You Will Say?
- What Happens When You Pray?
- Why Do Some Christians Choose Not To Pray?

Why Pray If God Already Knows What Will Happen?

What a great question. Prayer is counterintuitive. In what other situation do you ask for something or plead with someone when you know for certain their mind is already made up about what they will do? Psalm 115:3 (NIV) even tells us, "Our God is in heaven; He does whatever pleases Him."To understand all this, we need to think about what Christians call "the sovereignty of God." It's true that God already knows everything that will happen for the rest of eternity. He knows the big events and the small moments of each of our lives, and nothing is beyond His control. So it's a mistake to think of prayer as the way we change God's mind or alter His direction in a situation.

Prayer is a process through which we learn to trust God. He listens to us patiently. He takes our requests seriously. Then He considers everything in the context of the bigger picture only He can see. Pete Greig, the founder of the 24/7 Prayer movement, says, "In prayer, we use our will to come into agreement with God's will — 'Let your kingdom come.'"

God knows better than you do what the eventual outcomes of every situation will be. If you pray for dry weather for an outdoor event your church has planned, God might know of another reason why it needs to rain that day. It's easy to accept this idea when it does not affect a personal situation in your life, but the test of faith comes when God asks you to trust Him with something or someone that matters to you.

Why Pray If God Already Knows What You Will Say?

Because prayer is one of the main ways you develop a connection with God.

Again, this is a valid question. In the Bible, we read these words, You have searched me, LORD, and You know me. You know when I sit and when I rise; You perceive my thoughts from afar.

You discern my going out and my lying down; You are familiar with all my ways. Before a word is on my tongue You, LORD, know it completely. (Psalm 139:1-4, NIV).

If God knows what you are thinking, why is He so concerned about you talking to Him? Because prayer is one of the main ways you develop a connection with God. In prayer, you're talking with Him, not just to Him. The apostle Paul tells us, "Do not be anxious about anything, but in every situation, by prayer and petition, with thanksgiving, present your requests to God. And the peace of God, which transcends all understanding, will guard your hearts and your minds in Christ Jesus" (Philippians 4:6-7, NIV).

It's interesting that Paul does not say that when you bring your concerns to God, God will give you peace by explaining or resolving every situation you bring to Him. Instead, he suggests that the peace of God in your heart and mind is somehow more likely to satisfy you and ease your fears than if He fixed or explained everything immediately. Through prayer, you develop a trusting relationship with God. Over time, you also learn to recognize His voice as He speaks to you. The Bible clearly shows Him choosing to act in response to the prayers of His people.

Through prayer, God transforms your heart so that having your requests fulfilled becomes secondary to feeling truly known by God and precious to Him.

What Happens When You Pray?

Prayer is essential to the way He transforms you.

God invites you to pray in all circumstances. Prayer is essential to the way He transforms you, and the Bible encourages you that your prayers can have a powerful effect in the world. So what can you expect to see happen as you commit to praying regularly?

- **You will recognize that you are not God.** Every time it occurs to you to pray, you are saying, "In my own strength, I cannot do all that I want to do. I need something more, someone else."
- **You gain strength from God Himself.** Prayer is a way of inviting God to join you in life's struggles. You invite the Holy Spirit to do what He was placed within you to do.
- **You realize the world does not begin and end with you.**
  Being dependent on someone else to meet your needs is humbling. When infants cry or scream, someone usually comes and meets their needs. It's easy to allow prayer to become too focused on registering complaints or making requests (or demands). Whether you pray for yourself or another person, you acknowledge that someone else — God — is the center of the universe. You acknowledge that He needs to change something about you or the situations you are bringing to Him.

- **You surrender control to somebody else.** Everyone craves control to one degree or another. Some just believe they're better at being in control than others. Prayer allows you to admit to God that He belongs in the driver's seat of your life.
- **You communicate your real feelings about a situation.**

  Prayer creates a safe space to process your thoughts and feelings. Do you feel ready to give God control of your life? Do you feel safe being completely known by God, or does that make you feel exposed? You are under God's protection — in His safekeeping. Over time, as you pray, you will feel able to bring the real you to your moments with God.
- **You trust that God is with you.** Unless you are happy to admit that you talk to floors or ceilings, when you pray, you're believing that someone is listening. The more you trust in the presence of God's Holy Spirit as you pray, the more you will learn to trust Him with the outcomes.
- **You feel inspired to take steps of faith.**
- Perhaps you have a desire to be bolder in talking about what you believe. Or maybe you have a neighbor or colleague you feel God nudging you to

go deeper with. Praying for that person is a step of faith in itself, because God may invite you to be part of the answer to your own prayer. Explore what it means to take a step of faith.

- **The Bible shows God waiting to act in response to prayer.**
  God knows what He wants to do in the world and in our individual lives. He wants us to lean on Him in every situation, and He wants to change the world through us.
  "If you remain in Me and My words remain in you, ask whatever you wish, and it will be done for you. This is to My Father's glory, that you bear much fruit, showing yourselves to be My disciples" (*John 15:7-8,* NIV).

These are just a few of the outcomes when people come to God through prayer. As you choose to bring all your fears, hopes, ambitions and desires to God, you will see Him respond in ways that speak to you specifically.

So how does this sound to you? Scary? Intriguing? Exciting? Or utterly confusing? All of the above are natural responses. Prayer is a mysterious activity because, in prayer, you choose to humble yourself before someone you cannot literally see, hear or touch.

It's not surprising that many Christians struggle with prayer, then, and some of us go through seasons when we choose not to pray at all.

Why Do Some Christians Choose Not To Pray?

... worse still, gave you no sense that He'd even heard your prayer...and felt let down by God.

Here are just a few reasons why people sometimes decide not to pray — and what we think God wants to say to you if one of these reasons keeps you from praying.

FEAR OF DISAPPOINTMENT

Have you ever brought a need to God and felt like He did not do what you hoped He would or, worse still, gave you no sense that He'd even heard your prayer? You are not alone. God never promises to answer prayers the way you want Him to. But as you spend time with God by praying and reading the Bible, you will develop trust in Him. This trust guards your heart during times when you feel let down by God, or even angry with Him.

God is also completely willing to listen to you no matter how you feel about Him at that moment. Try reading Psalm 13 to discover what honest conversations with God sound like.

Struggling To Pray "The Right Way"

Do you ever try to pray but struggle with the feeling that you're doing something wrong? Maybe you do not feel as connected to God as you want to, or perhaps you just struggle with distraction. Even the 12 men who spent three years with Jesus — His disciples — had to ask Him to teach them how to pray. He answered by giving them a simple prayer that Christians the world over have been using ever since. You can read what's known as "the Lord's prayer" in Matthew 6:9-13. We have also created "How to Pray: A Beginner's Guide" to help you develop the habit of praying regularly and to refresh your time with God if you've already had that habit.

PRIDE

There's no getting away from the fact that sometimes you just want to do things in your own strength rather than relying on God. Human beings have a natural inclination to be prideful, wanting the credit for making things happen in their lives. When you pray, it can feel like you are being passive about something important — asking God to act while you do nothing. This feeling is not the truth. Prayer is about expressing our dependence on God's Holy Spirit to live the way God wants us to live. Jesus warned His disciples about trying to branch out and do things in their own strength:

> *If you remain in Me and I in you, you will bear much fruit; apart from Me you can do nothing. ... If you remain in Me and My words remain in you, ask whatever you wish, and it will be done for you. (John 15:5,7, NIV)*

Prayer is one of the most active things you can do as a Christian. It demonstrates that you are deciding to rely on God's strength and not your own. It also demonstrates your willingness to give Him all the credit when your prayers are answered. Your enemy, the devil, wants you to try to live in your own strength because he knows you will inevitably experience more failure that way. He knows those failures lead to disappointment that can turn into resentment toward God. His purpose is to break down your connection with God by whatever means possible. Exploiting your pride is one of his favorite tactics.

If you want your relationship with God to grow deeper over time, you need to communicate with Him regularly.

Learn more about what spiritual warfare looks like and what it means for your growth as a Christian.

The reasons people neglect or avoid prayer are understandable. Everyone experiences times when praying feels like too much hard work without any obvious reward. But if you want your relationship with God to grow deeper over time, you need to communicate with Him regularly. There are no rules about how many times each day or each week you need to pray if you want to see God respond. But the more time you spend with anyone, the more known and safe you will feel. The more you bring someone into the situations in your life that matter, the more you will understand how they think and respond. This is true of a friend or a spouse, and it's true of God our Father .God wants you to know Him in a way that transforms every aspect of who you are. Prayer is one of the ways He chooses to make that happen.

> *"Ask and it will be given to you; seek and you will find; knock and the door will be opened to you." (Matthew 7:7, NIV)*

Young Adult's Guide On How To Pray.

To pray means to communicate with God. That can mean thanking Him, praising Him, confessing something you've done wrong, or expressing a need you have. It can even mean just talking to Him as you would to a friend. Learning how to pray is really about developing a relationship with God. Relationships are built on moments of connection. Those moments of connection bond you to another person, and many of them center on communication — the words you say and the way you say them. But how do you do that with the God of the universe?

Prayer is a supernatural activity. What does that mean? Think about it for a moment. You are talking with a God who is unlike anyone else you could ever talk with. He has a personality and qualities you can understand and relate to, but you cannot expect to relate to God in exactly the way you might to a close friend or family member. He's so much bigger and more incredible than that. He is beyond what you can understand in the natural everyday world. He is supernatural.

Even if talking honestly with other people comes very naturally to you, it's understandable if talking with God feels like a steep learning curve .This is a practical guide to getting started talking with God, no matter where you are on your spiritual journey.

Some Questions We Will Answer:

- What Is Prayer?
- Why Should You Pray?
- How Do You Pray?
- What Should You Pray For?
- What Will Happen When You Pray?
- Ways to Develop Your Prayer Life

We hope that after reading this guide, you'll feel equipped for your journey with prayer. If you still have questions, please ask them in the comment section.

What Is Prayer?

People often say that prayer is just talking to God as you would to anyone else. It's true that a relationship with God contains many of the same ingredients as our other relationships. But there is at least one unique factor: we can't rely on the senses of sight, sound or touch to connect with God. So talking to God is just like relating to anyone else except in the ways it is completely different.

Perhaps the best place to begin is by making clear that prayer is more about talking with God than just talking to Him. What you believe about God and your relationship with Him is fundamental to how you will learn to talk with Him.

> *Faith is the essential ingredient if you want your prayer life to never lose its flavor.*

God is ready and willing to listen because He knows you and wants to be known by you. If you believe that, or you want to believe that, you're ready to learn how to pray.

Why Should You Pray?

People pray for all sorts of reasons. Some pray to comfort themselves in troubling times and to acknowledge there is a spiritual dimension to life. But Christians pray for very specific reasons.

Becoming a Christian is about much more than adopting a label, changing your demographic or subscribing to a new worldview. To be a Christian is to believe God invited you into a personal relationship with Him and to accept that invitation.

Saying that you can experience being a Christian in the way God intended without learning to pray is like saying you can be happily married or have a deep friendship without regular communication. But maybe the question is not why should Christians pray, but why should they want to?

Four Important Reasons Why You Might Choose To Pray As A Christian

- You want to tell God how much you love Him and why.
- You need to say "I'm sorry" for specific actions or attitudes.
- You want to thank God.
- You want to bring a concern about your life or someone in your life to God and invite Him to help.

If you have never really prayed before and you want to know what to say, these four reasons for prayer also provide a good template to start with. And if that's you, we want to share about more of the essentials before we go any further.

HOW DO YOU PRAY? So let's deal with the practical stuff.

What position should I be in to pray?

You can bow, kneel, stand or walk around when you pray. God will hear you whatever you do, so choose a position that helps you focus. Kneeling, or bowing your head, is a great way to focus your body and your mind on God. It's also a way to show how much you respect His authority.

What do I say?

Start by addressing God directly in a way that acknowledges the uniqueness of who He is.People will say things like, "Father God," "Heavenly Father" or "Almighty God." How you choose to address Him will remind you and anyone you might be praying with about who you are talking to and what He represents in your life.

Do I pray to God the Father, Jesus or the Holy Spirit?

This is completely up to you. Choose one or try praying to each member of the Trinity at different times, because they are all listening to you. If you are a Christian, the Holy Spirit is the presence of God living within you. So you can address Him directly with confidence that He is as close as He could be.

Note: Find out more about how to understand the Holy Spirit's role in your life.

Should I pray out loud?

Depending on how comfortable you feel or what kind of situation you are in, you will choose whether to pray out loud or silently. Over time, you will likely grow in your confidence praying out loud. If you are praying for someone who is physically present with you, it might encourage them to hear your faith expressed through your prayers. But if you find praying silently allows you to focus more on God than on someone you might be praying with, go for it. The one time most of us need to stop talking is when we are trying to listen to God. You will find it harder to hear what He is saying if you are doing all the talking.

When and where do I pray?

Anytime and anywhere can work, but it's good to find a distraction-free time and place if possible. God deserves your focused attention, and you might find it harder to listen to Him in a busy place. Some people create a space in their homes for this purpose, like a prayer closet. Others will choose a favorite park to take time out with God, or even a coffee shop.

How do I end a prayer?

A common way to end prayer is by saying something like, "In the name of Jesus, amen."

But why is this? Well, think about how you began your prayer by addressing God directly, by name. This is important because it acknowledges that God is more than a force, more than an unnamed higher power or an idea. God is a person choosing to be present in your life. Most importantly, He is the only person with the authority and ability to answer your prayers.

This common conclusion is a reminder of who this God is.

Whatever you choose to say can also act as a reminder that you believe God has heard your prayers and that you trust Him to know how best to answer them. If you're the kind of person who starts talking to God as you go about your day, you don't need to wrap up every communication with a formal ending for God to take you seriously. God is a Father who loves His children to talk to Him as much as possible.

What Should You Pray For?

Whatever is on your mind matters to God, because you matter to Him. As you develop the habit of praying, over time you will gain a sense of what things God is talking to you about and what He thinks is worth your attention. In the beginning, try not to get too hung up on what you should be praying about. God has all the time in the world, and He's far more patient with us than we are with ourselves.

But if you're ever in doubt, pray like Jesus.

Jesus' closest friends, the men he focused most of his attention on, faced the same problem we do. So they asked Jesus to teach them how to pray. The result is the best-known prayer in human history — what we call the Lord's Prayer.

> Our Father in heaven, hallowed be Your name, Your kingdom comes, Your will be done, on earth as it is in heaven. Give us today our daily bread. And forgive us our debts, as we also have forgiven our debtors. And lead us not into temptation, but deliver us from the evil one. (*Matthew 6:9-13*, N I V)

Looking at Jesus' prayer piece by piece provides some tracks for the prayer lives of His followers to run on.

Five Lessons On Prayer To Learn From The Example Jesus Gives Us:

1. **"Our Father in heaven, hallowed be Your name."** Jesus starts by establishing our identity as children of God. He is stressing the importance of really owning this belief as a source of confidence that when you pray, your Father in heaven will listen.
2. **"Your kingdom come, your will be done, on earth as it is in heaven."**
   It's tempting to start your prayers in a hurry, getting the formalities out of the way so you can get on with asking God for what you want or need. In contrast, Jesus makes a point about placing God's agenda before your own. He also uses this phrase as a reminder that what is true of God in heaven is also true here on earth, where we bring our needs to Him in prayer.
3. **"Give us today our daily bread."**
   No request is too big or too small for God but examine the motives behind whatever you ask Him for. Jesus knows that when you pray, you often focus on the things you want from God. He started out by focusing on God's will, and now he encourages you to think about what you really need from God today.
4. **"Forgive us our debts, as we forgive our debtors."**
   Forgiveness was at the heart of Jesus' teaching during His time on earth, and so we find it here at

the heart of His guide to prayer. Jesus first stresses your need to focus on asking forgiveness for anything you have done that displeases God. Second, He reminds you to search your heart for any unforgiveness you might feel toward another person and ask Him to help you release them from that debt. The debt could be something someone literally took from you; more often it will be some way in which you feel someone has hurt you.

5. **"Lead us not into temptation but deliver us from the evil one."**

   Finally, Jesus closes His prayer by encouraging us to keep in mind that the Christian life is a spiritual battle and we have a very real enemy. The fact that Jesus closes His prayer this way feels like a reminder about how natural and tempting humans find it to stray from God's protection.

Great Ideas and Knowledge to Learn from Jesus Prayer:

But this is just the beginning! There are plenty of things that the Bible suggests are on God's heart for you — things you can pray for at any time:

- Your connection with God growing deeper day by day.

- Anything in your life interfering with your intimacy with God.
- The people God wants you to express His love to.
- Your role as an ambassador for Jesus in the world.
- Your family.
- Your friends.
- Your career.
- How to steward the financial resources God has entrusted to you.
- Your understanding of the Bible.
- Developing the spiritual gifts you have been given through the Holy Spirit.

Why not start with this list and ask God to reveal what else He wants to talk with you about?

What Will Happen When You Pray?

Does trying to pray leave you feeling like you missed a class everyone else attended? The notion of a two-way conversation with a God you cannot literally see or hear can feel elusive and frustrating. We all spend years learning to read, write, add and subtract; relatively few people spend devoted time learning to pray.

One possible explanation for this is that we incorrectly think there is an ideal formula or playbook for prayer.

Remember, prayer is about a unique relationship between you and God. If you are recently married, you can learn a lot from couples who have been together for years. But their experiences will only get you so far.

Six Things to Expect as You Develop a Conversation with God:

1. **You will recognize that you are not God.**
   Every time you pray, you are saying, "In my own strength, I cannot do all that I want to do. I need something more, someone else."
2. **You will realize the world doesn't begin and end with you.**
   When babies cry, someone usually comes and meets their needs, but this kind of attention does not last forever. Growing up is a painful process of slowly coming to terms with the reality that the world doesn't revolve around you. Whether you are praying for yourself or others, you're acknowledging someone else is the center of the universe.
3. **You will gain strength from outside of yourself.**
   Prayer is a way of inviting a higher power to enter into your life's struggles. Prayer can be a source of strength, wisdom and inner peace.

4. **You will surrender control to somebody else.**
   Everyone is a control freak to one degree or another. Prayer allows you to admit to God that you need Him in the driver's seat of your life.
5. **You will communicate your real feelings.**
   Do you feel ready to give God control of your life? Talk to God honestly about how that question makes you feel. He knows everything about you. He's eager to listen 24/7. Prayer is a safe way to process your thoughts and feelings.
6. **You will trust that God is with you.**
   Unless you're happy to admit that you talk to floors or ceilings, when you pray, you're believing that someone or something is listening — and might even do something about the things you're talking about.

How Does This Sound to You? Scary? Intriguing? Utterly Confusing?

Prayer is a mysterious thing — simple but profound. Billions of people pray every day. What you can be sure of is that God listens to them all.

Ways To Develop Your Prayer Life

Think about someone praying. What are you picturing? Perhaps you imagine someone kneeling beside their bed and listing concerns or requests to God. Maybe you see someone sitting silently. You might even imagine a group of people all talking at the same time, making a holy ruckus as they pour their hearts out to a higher power. Whatever your picture, the crucial question is, do you see prayer as a monologue or a dialogue?

The majority of books on healthy relationships describe communication as the cornerstone. Most of them also make the point that the hardest part of communication isn't what you need to say, but how well you need to listen. Most of us never hear from God audibly. And yet many people claim God speaks to them. So how does that work? If you're looking for a formula to get God to talk when you need it most — you might be disappointed. But here are three ideas to try if you want to learn to hear from Him

Pray With a Journal

Others of us find that as we write out our prayers, our thoughts become clearer.

"Thoughts disentangle themselves when they pass through lips and fingertips." Dawson Trotman's words beautifully capture why journaling is a vital part of so many people's spiritual journeys. Some of us are verbal processors and praying out loud enables us to clearly communicate with God. Others of us find that as we write out our prayers, our thoughts become clearer. You could begin with a Bible verse that stands out to you, even if you don't know why it stands out to you.

Ask Yourself These Simple Questions as You Read A Bible Passage:

- What does this passage tell me about God?
- What feelings does this passage evoke in me and why?
- What thoughts or memories occur to me as I reflect on these verses?
- What could God want me to hear since this is what He gave me to read?

Answering these questions will help you reach a point where you can ask God how He wants you to respond to whatever you are reading. God wants to speak to you, and He's not limited by how good a listener you are. So don't rush yourself, but trust the Holy Spirit, who lives inside you and helps you learn to recognize God's voice.

Show God that you're willing to listen, and He'll show you He's able to speak.

NOTE: *Learn more about living in the power of the Holy Spirit.*

Take A Walk With God

Jesus' closest relationships on earth were built as He walked with people day after day. Men in particular often develop deep friendships doing things side by side rather than talking face to face. So why not schedule some time to connect with God the way you would with anyone else you value?

Pray With Other People

Listening to someone else talk with God can help you focus on Him. Think of someone you know who talks about God's tangible presence in their life. Ask if you can pray together. While time alone with God is vital to our spiritual growth, God Himself tells us that when two or more gather to focus on Him, something special happens (*Matthew 18:20*).

If you are praying in public or with another person, remember to talk to God and not them. It's easy to fall into the trap of saying what you think another Christian wants to hear rather than what you need to communicate to God.

Chapter Five: 150+ Prayer Points

PRAYER TO RECEIVE FRESH FIRE.

When you need personal revival.

When you need fresh fire for fighting the battles of life.

When you need the power of the Holy Spirit to enable fulfill your destiny in life.

Introduction.

Fire is one thing which the enemy cannot withstand; when you receive fresh fire, you become untouchable. When the totality of your life is set on fire, you will emerge a winner in the battles of life; the fire of the Holy Spirit is one weapon which we need for victory in life. God has promised to slay His enemy, who also is your enemy.

Fire is one of the weapons which God has freely given to you to enable you to go through life successfully. Whenever the fire of your life goes down, you will be enveloped with fear; but the moment your fire level increases, it will be victory all the way. The shortest route to your testimonies is to pray fresh fire upon your life. God dwells in the midst of fire; when God envelopes your life with fresh fire, His mighty presence will also envelopes your life. You need to pray these prayer points aggressively if you want to experience the fire of God afresh. Please, pray these prayer points aggressively and the God who answereth by fire shall manifest Himself in your life.

- And call ye on the name of your gods, and I will call on the name of the LORD: and the God that answereth by fire, let him be God. And all the people answered and said, it is well spoken. **1Kings 18:24.**

- For by fire and by his sword will the lord plead with all flesh; and the slain of the LORD shall be many. **Isaiah 66:16.**
- Christ hath redeemed us from the curse of the law, being made a curse for us; for it is written, curse is every one that hangeth on a tree: That the blessing of Abraham might come on the gentiles through Jesus Christ; that we might receive the promise of the spirit through faith. **Galatians 3:13-14.**
- And the Lord shall deliver from every evil work, and will preserve me unto His heavenly kingdom; to whom be glory forever and ever, amen**. 2Timothy 4:18.**
- Who hath delivered us from the power of darkness, and hath translated us into the kingdom of His dear son. **Colossians 1:13.**
- And having spoiled principalities and powers, He made a show of them openly, triumphing over them in it. **Colossians 2:15.**

Aggressive Praise/Worship – (30 Minutes).

Make A Declaration or Confession.

Prayer Points – Part 1

- Thank God for His mighty power to save to the uttermost and for the power to deliver from any form of bondage.
- Confess your sins and those of your ancestors, especially those sins linked to evil powers and idolatry.
- I cover myself with the blood of Jesus.
- I release myself from any inherited bondage and limitation, in the name of Jesus.
- O, Lord, send your axe of fire to the foundation of my life, and destroy every veil plantation therein.
- Blood of Jesus, flush out from my system, every inherited satanic deposit, in the name of Jesus.
- Any rod of the wicked, rising up against my family line, be rendered impotent for my sake, in the name of Jesus.
- I cancelled the consequences of any evil local name attached to my person, in the name of Jesus.
- You evil foundational plantations, come out of my life with all your roots, in the name Jesus.
- I break and loose myself from every form of demonic bewitchment, in the name of Jesus.
- I release myself from every evil domination and control, in the name of Jesus.

- I release myself the grip of any problem transferred into my life from the womb, in the name of Jesus.
- Blood of Jesus and the fire of the Holy Spirit, cleanse every organ in my body, in the name of Jesus.
- I break and loose myself from every inherited evil covenant, in the name of Jesus.
- I break and lose myself from every inherited evil curse, in the name of Jesus.
- I vomit every evil consumption that I have been fed with as a child, in the name of Jesus.
- I command all foundational strongmen attached to my life to be paralyzed, in the name of Jesus.
- Lord, let the blood of Jesus be transfused into my blood vessels, in the name of Jesus.
- Every gate, opened to the enemy by my foundation, be closed forever with the blood of Jesus.
- Lord Jesus, walk back into every second of my life and deliver me where I need deliverance; heal me where I need healing and transform me where I need transformation.
- Thou power in the blood of Jesus, separate me from the sins of my ancestors.
- Blood of Jesus remove any unprogressive label from every aspect of my life.

- Lord, create in me a clean heart by your power.
- Lord, let the anointing of the Holy Spirit break every yoke of backwardness in my life.
- Lord, renew a right spirit within me.
- Lord, teach me to die to self.
- Thou brush of the lord, scrub out every dirtiness in my spiritual pipe, in the name of Jesus.
- Lord, ignite my calling with your fire.
- Lord, anoint me to pray without ceasing.
- Lord, establish me as a holy person unto you.
- Lord, restore my spiritual eyes and ears.
- Lord, let the anointing to excel in my spiritual and physical life fall on me.
- Lord, produce in me the power of self-control and gentleness.
- Holy Spirit, breath on me now, in the name of Jesus.
- Holy Spirit fire, ignite me to the glory of God.
- Lord, let every rebellion flee from my heart.
- I command every spiritual contamination in my life to receive cleansing by the blood of Jesus.
- Every rusted spiritual pipe in my life, receive wholeness, in the name of Jesus.
- I command every power, eating up my spiritual pipe, to be roasted, in the name of Jesus.

- I renounce any evil dedication placed upon my life, in the name of Jesus.
- I break every evil edict and ordination, in the name of Jesus.
- Lord, cleanse every soiled parts of my life.
- Lord, deliver me from every foundational pharaoh.
- Lord, heal every wounded parts of my body.
- Lord, bend every evil rigidity in my life.
- Lord, re-align every satanic straying in my life.
- Lord, let the fire of the Holy Spirit every satanic freeze in my life.
- lord, give me a life that kills death.
- lord, kindle me with the fire of charity.
- Lord, glue me together where I am opposed to myself.
- Lord, enrich me with your gifts.
- Lord, quicken me and increase my desire for the things of heaven.
- By your rulership, O Lord, let the lust of the flesh in my life die.
- Lord Jesus, increase daily in my life.
- Lord Jesus, maintain your gifts in my life.
- Lord. Refine and purge my life, by your fire
- Holy Spirit, inflame my heart with your fire, in the name of Jesus.

- Holy Ghost fire, begin to burn away every power of the bond woman in me, in the name of Jesus.
- Lord, make me ready to go wherever you send me.
- Lord Jesus, never let me shut you out.
- Lord Jesus, work feely in me and through me.
- Begin to thank God for answers to your prayers.

Provoking The Baptism of Fire.

One of the greatest weapons for crushing oppression is to be baptized with the fire of the Holy Ghost.

Generally, oppression will thrive where there is no fire. The devil and his agents will perpetrate all kinds of wicked acts when they find the atmosphere comfortable. You cannot say no to oppression until you have fire in your life. When you become baptized in the fire of the Holy Ghost, your life will become too hot for the enemy to handle. If you have noticed symbols of oppression, intimidation, manipulation and wickedness, it is an indication of the fact that your fire has been extinguished. Rather than box shadows, you need to go back to the presence of God and receive fresh fire. The baptism of fire is a symbol of the overflowing presence of the Holy Spirit in your life.

The moment you are endued with fire from on high, you will become master over circumstances and forces of darkness. This prayer section will restore your lost glory and make you to declare that there is something in your life that can repel the enemy. The fire of the Holy Ghost is the antidote for rescuing a perpetual candidate of satanic attack.

This prayer program is for those who have labored under negative anointing at one time or the other; But when you are baptized by the fire of the Holy Ghost, it's presence will consume and expel every form of negative anointing in your life.

Baptism by fire will exert a sanitizing influence upon your life. One simple way of carrying out thorough internal environmental sanitation is to seek baptism by fire if you have never experienced it. If you have sensed in any way that your fire level is low, you need a refreshing experience of fresh baptism in the Holy Ghost. You need to seek God's face for baptism by fire. These prayers will thoroughly eliminate every stranger hibernating in your life.

Aggressive Praise/Worship – (30 Minutes)

Make A Declaration or Confession.

Scriptures: ***John 12:24; 2Cor. 6; 1Cor. 9:16; Deut28:13; Rom. 8:35-39.***

Prayer Points – Part 2.

- Thank God for the privilege of your calling.
- Thank the lord for the power of the Holy Spirit.
- Make confession of sins and repent.
- Father let the Holy Spirit fill me afresh.
- Father, let every unbroken areas of my life be broken, in the name of Jesus.
- Father, incubate me with the fire of the Holy Spirit, In Jesus name.
- Every anti-power bondage in my life, break, in Jesus name.
- O Lord, let all strangers flee from my spirit and let the Holy Spirit take control, in the name of Jesus.
- Lord, catapult my spiritual life to the mountaintop.
- Father, let heaven open and let the glory of God fall upon me, in the name of Jesus.
- Father, let signs and wonders be my lot, in the name of Jesus.

- Every joy of the oppressors upon my life be turned into sorrow, in the name of Jesus.
- All multiple strong men operating against me, be paralyzed in the name of Jesus.
- Lord, open my eyes and ears to receive wondrous things from you.
- Lord, ignite my spiritual life so that I will stop fishing in unprofitable waters.
- Lord, release your tongue of fire upon my life and burn away all spiritual filthiness present within me.
- Father, make me to hunger and thirst for righteousness in the name of Jesus.
- Lord, help me to be ready to do your work without expecting any recognition from others.
- Lord, give me victory over emphasizing the weaknesses and sin of other people, while ignoring my own.
- Lord, give me depth and root in my faith.
- Lord, heal every area of backsliding in my spiritual life.
- Lord, help me to be willing to serve others rather than wanting to exercise authority.
- Lord, open my understanding concerning the scriptures.

- Lord, help me to live each day recognizing that the day will come when you will judge secret lives and innermost thoughts.
- Lord, let me be willing to be the clay in your hands, ready to molded as you desire.
- Lord, wake me up from any form of spiritual sleep and help me to put on the armour of light.
- Lord, give me victory over all carnality and help me to be at center of your will.
- I stand against anything in my life that will cause others to stumble, in the name of Jesus Christ.
- Lord, help me put away childish things and put on maturity.
- Lord, empower me to stand firm against all the schemes and techniques of the devil.
- Lord, give me a big appetite for the pure milk and solid food in your word.
- Lord, empower me to stay away from anything or anybody, who might take God's place in my heart.
- Lord I thank you for the testimonies that will follow.
- I declare that I am called of God, no evil power shall cut me down in the name of Jesus,
- Lord, give me the power to be faithful to my calling, in the name of Jesus.

- I receive the anointing to remain steady, committed, and consistent in my ministerial life in Jesus name.
- I declare that I shall not be lured in politics, church rivalry or rebellion, in the name of Jesus.
- Lord, give me the wisdom to respect my teachers and seniors who have trained me, in the name of Jesus.
- Lord, give me the heart of a servant so that I can experience your blessings every day, in the name of Jesus.
- I receive power to rise with wings as eagles, in the name of Jesus.
- I decree that the enemy will not waste my calling, in the name of Jesus.
- By the power of the lining God, the devil will not swallow my ministerial destiny, in the name of Jesus.
- Power for effective development in my calling, come upon me now, in the name of Jesus.
- I declare war against spiritual ignorance, in the name of Jesus.
- I bind and cast out every un teachable spirit in the name of Jesus.
- I receive the anointing for success in my ministry, in the name of Jesus.

- I shall not be an enemy of integrity, in the name of Jesus.
- I shall not steal God's money, in the name of Jesus.
- I shall not disgrace the call of God upon my life, in Jesus name.
- I shall walk in holiness every day, in Jesus name.
- I bind the spirit of sexual immorality, in Jesus name.
- I receive the culture of loyalty in my ministry, in the name of Jesus.
- I shall not become an old king that is resistant to advice, in the name of Jesus.
- I shall not live a wasteful and extravagant life, in the name of Jesus.
- I shall not serve my wonderful savior for filthy financial gain. In the name of Jesus.
- I prevent every spirit of quarrel and opposition from my wife/husband, in the name of Jesus.
- My wife/husband shall not scatter my church members, in the name of Jesus.
- Every Judas in my ministry, fall into your trap, in the name of Jesus.
- My ministry will not destroy my marriage, in the name of Jesus.
- My marriage will not destroy my ministry, in the name of Jesus.

- My children will not become misfired arrows in my ministry, in the name of Jesus.
- I c1laim progress and excellence for my ministry, in the name of Jesus.
- My church shall experience prosperity, in the name of Jesus.
- Lord, let my ministry reach the un-reached, in the name of Jesus.
- A multitude of people will go to heaven because of my ministry, in the name of Jesus.
- I kill every attack on my ministry; I shall prevail, in the name of Jesus.
- I shall not bite the fingers that fed me, in the name of Jesus.
- I shall not engage in rebellion, in the name of Jesus.
- Every power of my father's house working against my calling, die, in the name of Jesus.
- Anointing for excellence fall upon me, in the name of Jesus.
- Lord, break me and re-mould me, in the name of Jesus.
- I will not surrender to the enemy, in the name of Jesus.
- I shall not die before my time, in the name of Jesus.
- I shall not covet the prosperity of Na'aman, in the name of Jesus.

- Let God arise and let every enemy of calling scatter, in the name of Jesus.
- I receive fresh fire and fresh anointing, in the name of Jesus.
- Father, let your fire that byrns every deposit of the enemy fall upon me, in the name of Jesus.
- Holy Ghost fire, incubate me, in the name of the Lord Jesus Christ.
- I reject any evil stamp or seal placed upon me by ancestral spirits, in the name of Jesus.
- I release myself from every negative anointing, in the name of Jesus.
- Every door of spiritual leakage, close, in the name of Jesus.
- I charge every organ of my body with the fire of the Holy Spirit
- (*Methodically lay your right hand on various parts of your body beginning from the head*) in the name of Jesus.
- Every human spirit attacking my spirit, release, in the name of Jesus.
- I reject every spirit of the tail, in the name of Jesus.
- Sing the song "Holy Ghost fire, fire fall on me."
- All evil marks on my body, be burnt off by the fire of the Holy Spirit, in the name of Jesus.

- The anointing of the Holy Ghost, fall upon me and break every negative yoke, in the name of Jesus.
- Every garment of hindrance and dirtiness, be dissolved by the fire of the Holy Ghost.
- All my chained blessings, be released, in the name of Jesus.
- All spiritual cages inhibiting my progress, roast by the fire of the Holy Ghost, in the name of Jesus.

IX. Conclusions.

So far, we have learned more from the three stories in the three chapters of this book in a new dimension which we may not have considered to be of importance to our individual lives as it relates to the residual power in our mouths. The interesting story about the contest between the prophets of Baal and God's only prophet who withstood the numerous false prophets, thereby establishing that 'one with God is in majority' is a fact. Secondly, it demonstrates that God's power can rest on anybody who makes himself available to be used by God. There were more than seven hundred prophets of God in Israel at the time, but only Elijah made himself available; the rest went into hiding because of the fear of the king, the queen, and the princes in Israel.

This same power display was duplicated in the story of the 'army captains and their fifty troops', which goes further to confirm that God can release His power through man to accomplish whatever He wants to do, including healings, blessings, deliverances, salvation, miracles, empowerments, fighting battles and winning wars etc; these and other things will God do through any man who partners with Him, by strict discipline, obedience, trust, and faith. These are the character traits the book projected through the various story lines, of which every one of us are expected to covet and appropriate to become our lifestyle.

We will not forget to mention the pronouncement (i.e., spoken word of command against disobedience) of the man of God on the teenagers who mocked him. It demonstrates that there is power in the spoken word to bless or to curse; this time, it was used to curse. This same mouth was used to bless the cursed water of Jericho some few hours most probably. What we must learn here is this, we should realize that this same power is present within us if we cooperate with God as we draw nearer to Him; though we can do nothing on our own.

There are glaring evidence from the stories we have read so far that, for as long as man draw close to God, he would be endued with power to perform and act on behalf of God because all we need to live our lives has been packaged for us; what we have to do, is to draw on the available resources that has been divinely provided. In most cases, this is done through prayer.

The place of prayer cannot be over-emphasized here because it is one of the best-known methods made available by God to man for him to approach Him. The issue of 'why should man pray when God has already known everything about him'? Apart from approaching God when we are in need, God needed man most in communion fellowship than man's personal needs; it is at this communion table that He releases His power into our spirit, soul, and body. Prayer is the connecting rod between God and Man; that is why a prayer less man is a powerless man. Elijah and Elisha as demonstrated in this book are epitome of men of prayer and fasting; there are many great men and women in the scriptures who were given to prayers. Also, there are great men and women God is using today who have given themselves to prayers too; and you are encouraged to learn from such examples, both in scriptures and in our today's world.

Great efforts have been exerted to put together some scriptural prayer points that would assist the reader to join the queue of prayer warriors. At the time you prayerfully complete praying the prayer points in this book, a new leaf in your life would have been opened; a new life characterized by confidence, courage, boldness, strong faith, and abundant testimonies.

HAPPY READING.

Recommendations.

Ignorance has been recognized as one of the major obstacles that man must conquer in order to get to his destination; up till this moment, man still wallow in it. Most people play down on religion, but most religions tried to prove that man must be connected to his maker (God) in order to experience a blossom life on this planet earth. The scriptures say, my people perish because of lack of vision, knowledge, understanding, and probably wisdom; yet we still find some struggling against fate. It is time to wise- up.

Man cannot do much without his maker; this is a truth, and also a fact we should embrace. The entire book portrays a direct relationship with God to enable power flow to man for sustainability of his life; this connection is absolutely required by man because absolute power belongs to God. The book is leading and redirecting man's footsteps back to his maker for re-equipment, and rejuvenation for a better life. So, this book is exactly a starter-pack for a man who truly wants to regain lost grounds.

Finally, this writing is different from all other formal books on this topic, rather, it is a radical approach to gaining grounds rapidly from our common enemy who has deceived us to believe that we are powerless so that he can continue to afflict and project against us at will; but today you have come to know that there is power in your mouth to quench all the arrows shot at you.

I admonish you to put up your faith, obedience, commitment to begin the new journey to exercise the in-born talents and gifts which God has deposited in you from the beginning, even before you were born into this world. You were born a champion from the on-set. This book will enable you to realize yourself; just read meditatively and solemnly.

About the Author

Patrick Onorie is the presiding Bishop cum General Overseer of Christ Heritage Ministries with headquarters located in the city of Port Harcourt, Rivers State, Nigeria.

He holds a Bachelor of Theology (B.Th) in Biblical Ministries (1999), from LIFE Theological Seminary, Ikorodu, Lagos, Nigeria; an affiliate of LIFE Bible College, Los Angeles, USA.

He was awarded an honorary Doctor of Philosophy (PhD) degree in Management Science (2011) by Trinity College, Seychelles.

He holds also, a Doctor of Science (DSc) degree in Theology and Public Policy (2021) from the American Trinity University, California, USA.

He acted as General Overseer of Cornerstone Christian Church Inc., with headquarters in Agbarho-Warri, Delta State, Nigeria at the demise of the incumbent founder/ G.O, from November 2019 to December 2020.

OTHER BOOKS BY THE SAME AUTHOR

www.ingramcontent.com/pod-product-compliance
Lightning Source LLC
LaVergne TN
LVHW050316160826
845677LV00014B/3427

* 9 7 9 8 3 5 1 1 2 9 6 9 3 *